UPDOG

BTS

K-POP FAN FAVORITES

Heather E. Schwartz

Lerner Publications ◆ Minneapolis

Lerner Publications Company
An imprint of Lerner Publishing Group, Inc.
241 First Avenue North
Minneapolis, MN 55401 USA

For reading levels and more information, look up this title at www.lernerbooks.com.

Main body text set in ITC Franklin Gothic Std.
Typeface provided by Adobe Systems.

Designer: Viet Chu

Library of Congress Cataloging-in-Publication Data

Names: Schwartz, Heather E., author.
Title: BTS : K-pop fan favorites / Heather E. Schwartz.
Description: Minneapolis : Lerner Publications, 2023. | Series: In the spotlight (Updog books) | Includes bibliographical references and index. | Audience: Ages 8–11 | Audience: Grades 4–6 | Summary: "Boy band sensation BTS has taken the world by storm. These K-pop icons known for catchy music and intelligent lyrics have a fascinating story that readers will love digging into!"— Provided by publisher.
Identifiers: LCCN 2021051015 (print) | LCCN 2021051016 (ebook) | ISBN 9781728458359 (library binding) | ISBN 9781728463667 (paperback) | ISBN 9781728461762 (ebook)
Subjects: LCSH: BTS (Musical group)—Juvenile literature. | Rock musicians—Korea (South)—Biography—Juvenile literature. | Boy bands—Korea (South)—Juvenile literature.
Classification: LCC ML3930.B89 S25 2022 (print) | LCC ML3930.B89 (ebook) | DDC 782.4216/3095195 [B]—dc23

LC record available at https://lccn.loc.gov/2021051015
LC ebook record available at https://lccn.loc.gov/2021051016

Manufactured in the United States of America
2-1008901-50201-9/15/2022

TABLE OF CONTENTS

Beginnings

The crowd cheered as BTS took the Grammy Awards stage. Their harmonies sounded amazing!

harmony: different notes sung at the same time

BTS started in South Korea in 2010.
It had one member, rapper RM.

Suga and J-Hope joined as rappers too. Jung Kook, V, Jimin, and Jin joined as singers.

Each member brought their own personality.

UP NEXT!

Making it.

Fame!

BTS released their first album,
2 Cool 4 Skool, in 2013.

At first, they weren't very popular.

But their fans grew. A fan
club formed around them.

The club is called the ARMY. It stands for Adorable Representative M.C. for Youth.

STAR STATS

Full name: Bangtan Sonyeondan
(Bulletproof Boy Scouts)

Date formed: 2010

Home country: South Korea

HONORS:

In 2017, BTS was the first K-pop group to win a *Billboard* Music Award.

In 2020, they were the first K-pop artists to perform at the Grammy Awards.

They earned a Guinness World Record for most viewers (756,000) for a music concert livestream. The concert was "Bang Bang Con: The Live" in 2020.

Over time, the band members grew more true to themselves. They wrote smart, personal lyrics.

personal: relating to a person's private thoughts and feelings

BTS also developed a unique look. They are known for their matching outfits and colorful hair.

UP NEXT!

Superstar status.

ARMY Strong

In 2015, the band released *The Most Beautiful Moment in Life, Pt. 1.* It was a smash hit!

In 2018, they became the first South Korean band to hit No. 1 on the US *Billboard* 200 chart.

BTS was even named the world's best-selling artists of 2020. But they care about more than fame.

They support charities. They make connections with fans.

BTS loves spreading joy through music!

Just like BTS

BTS found success by being true to themselves. What's a goal of yours? How could being true to yourself help you reach it?

GLOSSARY

harmony: different notes sung at the same time

personal: relating to a person's private thoughts and feelings

unique: special or unusual

CHECK IT OUT!

BTS Official Website
https://ibighit.com/bts/eng/

National Geographic Kids: South Korea
https://kids.nationalgeographic.com/geography/countries
/article/south-korea

One in an ARMY
https://www.oneinanarmy.org

Schwartz, Heather E. *Harry Styles: Pop Star with an X Factor*. Minneapolis: Lerner Publications, 2023.

Sprinkel, Katy. *The Big Book of BTS: The Deluxe Unofficial Bangtan Book*. Chicago: Triumph Books, 2019.

York, M. J. *Learn Korean Words*. Mankato, MN: Child's World, 2020.

INDEX

PHOTO ACKNOWLEDGMENTS

Image credits: Theo Wargo/Getty Images, p. 4; Jeon Heon
-Kyun/EPA-EFE/Shutterstock.com, pp. 5–6; Geisler-Fotopress
GmbH/Alamy Stock Photo, p. 7; Seokyong Lee/Penta Press/
Shutterstock.com, pp. 8–9; AP Photo/John Nacion/STAR
MAX/IPx, p. 10; Rachel Luna/Stringer/Getty Images, p. 11;
Efren Landaos/SOPA Images/Shutterstock.com, p. 12; The
Chosunilbo JNS/Imazins/Getty Images, p. 14; Sara Jaye Weiss/
Shutterstock.com, p. 15; Ilgan Sports/Multi-Bits/Getty Images,
p. 16; Rob Latour/Shutterstock.com, p. 17; JTBC PLUS/Imazins/
Getty Images, p. 18; John Salangsang/Shutterstock.com, p. 19;
John Palmer/MediaPunch Inc./Alamy Stock Photo, p. 20. Design
elements: Medesulda/Getty Images; oxygen/Getty Images.

Cover: Efren Landaos/SOPA Images/Shutterstock.com.